W9-AVL-849

J
757.0973 Fisher, Leonard
Fis         Everett.
            The limners.

# *The* LIMNERS

*Portrait of Alice Mason, by an unknown artist. Oil, 1670. (Adams National Historic Site)*

COLONIAL CRAFTSMEN

# The
# LIMNERS

*America's Earliest Portrait Painters*

WRITTEN & ILLUSTRATED BY

*Leonard Everett Fisher*

**B**ENCHMARK **B**OOKS

MARSHALL CAVENDISH
NEW YORK

MOORESTOWN LIBRARY
111 W. Second Street
Moorestown, NJ 08057-2481

J
757.0973
Fis

Benchmark Books
Marshall Cavendish Corporation
99 White Plains Road
Tarrytown, NY 10591-9001

Copyright © 1969 by Leonard Everett Fisher

First Marshall Cavendish edition 2000

All rights reserved. No part of this book may be reproduced or utilized in any from
or by any means electronic or mechanical including photocopying, recording,
or by any information storage and retrieval system, without permission form
the copyright holders.

Library of Congress Cataloging-in-Publication Data
Fisher, Leonard Everett.
The limners: America's earliest portrait painters / written and illustrated by Leonard
Everett Fisher.
p. cm. — (Colonial craftsmen)
Includes index.
Summary: Discusses the motivation, materials, and techniques of the first "artists" in
colonial America—the sign painters—and how their works contribute to a better
understanding of early American history and society.
ISBN 0-7614-0932-7
1. Portrait painting, American—Juvenile literature. [1. Portrait painting, American. 2.
Artists. 3. Art, American—History] I. Title. II. Series: Fisher, Leonard Everett. Colonial
craftsmen.
ND1311.F5   1999   757'.0973—dc21   99-33369   CIP

Printed and bound in the United States of America

1   3   5   6   4   2

Other titles in this series
═══════════

THE ARCHITECTS
THE BLACKSMITHS
THE CABINETMAKERS
THE DOCTORS
THE GLASSMAKERS
THE HOMEMAKERS
THE PEDDLERS
THE PRINTERS
THE SCHOOLMASTERS
THE SHIPBUILDERS
THE SHOEMAKERS
THE SILVERSMITHS
THE WEAVERS
THE WIGMAKERS

═══════════

*Portrait of James Badger, by his grandfather, Joseph Badger (1708-1765). Oil on canvas, c. 1760. (Metropolitan Museum of Art, Rogers Fund)*

*Colonial signs*

A person walking down a street in a Colonial American town might have seen a variety of pictures. He might pass the Dancing Bear Tavern. Jutting out over the road in front of it would be a sign with the name of the place and a picture of a handsome brown bear, merrily jigging. Next to the tavern might be the bootmaker's shop, marked by a gilded sign in the shape of a boot; then the wigmaker's, with a wooden sign picturing the head of a grand gentleman in an elaborate white wig. Flapping in the wind in front of the Lion Tavern might be a bright picture of an impressive roaring lion, his mouth wide open, his tail lashing. Other places of business would have their picture signs, too.

In Colonial America, painted signs were an important part of everyday life. Because not everyone could read, a hand-lettered sign on a place of business was often useless. So it was the custom to hang out a sign with a picture on it — a picture that would attract attention and tell a story. A new sign always aroused a great deal of interest, and people looked at it as critically as a person today might view an important artist's latest work. Businessmen took pride in their signs.

Sign painting was almost an art. It took special skills. To be a good sign painter, a man had to be able to draw with a steady hand; he had to have some sense of color and shape and design; and he had to know how to mix paints and use them.

But sign painting alone was not enough to earn a man a living; he had to find other kinds of work, too. Sign painting was often a sideline, done in a person's spare time. By the middle of the seventeenth century, however, the colonies had grown and were prosperous enough so that a painter could find a variety of painting jobs to do. Besides making signs, a man might color the walls of a house, inside or outside; paint coaches and decorate them with coats of arms or other pictures; and even paint the designs for gravemarkers. He usually learned his trade by working for a number of years as an apprentice, or helper, to an experienced painter-stainer, or house painter.

There was another, more profitable occupation for the more ambitious painters. They became

*A page from a fifteenth-century illuminated manuscript, The Belles Heures of Jean, Duke of Berry. The picture shows St. Louis, King of France, on his way to the Holy Land. (Metropolitan Museum of Art, Cloisters Collection)*

*limners* (LIM-ners). The limners were the nearest thing to artists that existed in early Colonial America. They painted likenesses of people. Today few of their names are known, but some of their work still exists.

The work of a limner was called *limning* (LIM-ning). The words "limner" and "limning" were derived from an old English word for "drawing," or making pictures and designs with lines. At times, limning also meant "painting," using brushes and colors to make pictures or designs. In turn, the old English word came from a Latin word, *illuminare*, which meant "to make bright," "to light up," "to embellish." And during the late Middle Ages, before the invention of movable type and the printing press, limning came to mean "manuscript illumination," or the art of painting brightly colored designs on the parchment pages of hand-lettered, hand-bound books.

Manuscript illumination was very exacting work. The designs created were small and intricate. The medieval illuminators were required to render these tiny, complicated shapes with brilliant colors, painted flatly — that is, with no nat-

Rex egregie con
dam rex francie
ludouice pie cum rege glo
rie triumphans hodie pro

pace requie regni eterne
xpm deprecare. Vers.
Ora pro nobis beate
ludouice. Responsorium.

*Mrs. Elizabeth Freake and Baby Mary (probably painted in 1674), by an unknown artist. (Worcester Art Museum)*

ural shading at all. The various parts of the design — people, animals, buildings, flowers, and trees — did not look quite real. The objects were without shadows cast by light; they looked as if they existed in some kind of spaceless place that did not know the warm glow of the sun, the dark chill of the night, or the gray dampness of a rainy day.

While their pictures were much larger and simpler than those on the manuscripts, the sign painters inherited the same way of dealing with objects and colors. Their signs were flatly painted in brilliant hues, without any suggestion of shading.

As the colonists of America became prosperous and had a little more leisure time they began to seek ways to brighten their hardworking lives. They bought a few more luxuries; they wore clothes that were less sober; and they became interested in owning portraits of themselves and their families to hang on the walls and to pass along to their children or to send back to their relatives in the old country. There were no really trained portrait painters or artists in the colonies in the early times, so it was only natural that the sign painters, who were somewhat skilled in draw-

*Seventeenth-century portrait painters in Europe showed much more understanding of light and shadow than the limners did. Portrait of Robert Rich, Earl of Warwick, by Anthony Van Dyck (1599-1641). Oil on canvas. (Metropolitan Museum of Art, Jules S. Bache Collection)*

ing objects and using colored paints, should try their hand at making portraits. Other artisans who had some skill at drawing and painting became limners, too, in their spare time. All these men performed the task that photographers and portrait painters do today: they made pictures of people.

By the time the painters started their portrait work in America, truly great artists were creating magnificent oil portraits in Europe. Their work showed an understanding of light and shadow, and the people they painted looked rounded and three-dimensional and alive. The flat, bright figures of medieval art now seemed awkward and clumsy to Europeans. Limning continued to mean drawing and painting, but now it also came to mean any type of flatly painted picture or design done by a skilled artisan rather than by a gifted artist.

Soon limning no longer applied to manuscript illumination at all. Fewer manuscripts were being made and decorated by hand as more and more books were being printed on presses and illustrated with pictures cut on wood blocks. The men who still worked at decorating manuscript pages

*Portrait of Rev. John Davenport, by John Foster (?).*
*Oil on canvas, 1670. (Yale University Art Gallery)*

with flat, brilliantly colored designs began to call themselves illuminators.

The early work of the Colonial limners — the so-called "face painters" — shows many of the same qualities that the Colonial painted signs do. The shapes pictured are simple; the bodies of the people are stiff and badly proportioned and are usually posed in a very set way, possibly with the left arm folded across the chest and the right hand outflung. And the colors are painted flatly with little or no shading. Many of the pictures look as if the artist had drawn the outlines of the bodies, then had filled them in with color.

Sometimes the clothes are simple, but at other times they are elaborate and the lace and ribbons of the women are carefully painted. Perhaps the women actually wore clothes like this, or perhaps the limner created them in his imagination because they made a more decorative portrait.

The faces of the portraits are the interesting part. They are often crudely painted, with blank, set, unlifelike expressions. The children portrayed often do not look particularly like children. Moreover, they appear to have the same lifeless stare

*Portrait of Ann Pollard, by an unknown artist. Oil, 1721.*
*(Massachusetts Historical Society)*

as their painted elders. But all the portraits do look as if the limner had struggled to make a genuine likeness of the person he was painting, even though he usually lacked the skill and artistic knowledge to do it.

Today the simple, almost primitive pictures of the limners, unskillful though they sometimes are, seem somehow to express the times during which they were made. And some of them do this very vividly.

One of the portraits, painted around 1721, is of Ann Pollard, a Boston woman who had been a tavern keeper. At the time the picture was painted she was about one hundred years old, had 103 descendants, and was the only person living who had landed in Boston in 1630 with the original English settlers. She loved to recall how, as a little girl, she had been the first to leap from the landing boat to the shore. No one knows who the limner who painted her portrait was, but somehow he caught the flavor and character of this shrewd old woman so that she comes sharply alive for us even today.

Usually, for his paints, a limner either imported

dry powdered colors from England or purchased them from a house painter. These dry colors had to be prepared, or made "wet," in order to be usable for painting. A limner who liked to prepare his own paints poured the powdered color onto a smooth grindstone, a little at a time. Each time he poured the color, he added a few drops of an oil made from flaxseed, called linseed oil. As he did this he ground the color into a fine paste with a stone grinder, or *muller*, until the paint became smooth and buttery.

Some limners did not bother to grind their own paints. Instead, they bought their colors already prepared, from a house painter. These paints were usually small amounts that had been scraped from a paint mill in which the house painter was preparing a large quantity of color for someone's wall. This mill was made of a large stone trough or basin and a heavy stone ball. The painter slowly poured his dry color into the trough and added linseed oil. As he did this he rolled the heavy stone ball back and forth until the mixture of color and oil became a smooth paste.

Before the craftsman added turpentine to turn

the paste into a liquid house paint, however, he scraped the thick colored mixture from the ball or trough for the limner's use. These scrapings were still not fine enough for painting pictures; if they were not ground much finer, the limner found them difficult if not impossible to work with.

Some of the colors used by the house painters and sign painters were also used by the limners in making their portraits. One of these colors was Dutch pink. Strangely enough, Dutch pink was neither Dutch nor pink. It was a liquid yellow dye made from ripe buckthorn berries. In order to give the dye body, it was added to certain whitish pigments that had no coloring power of their own. Dutch pink may have been fashionable and useful as a house or sign paint, but it was worthless for painting portraits because it faded too quickly.

Another color the limners and painters used was a strong, dark blue-green called Prussian blue. It became popular in the colonies after 1725. Prussian blue was a poor color to use alone, since in time it turned brown or faded away altogether, but it was good as a tint to be combined with other colors.

Some other paints were of excellent quality. Among the colors were Indian red (a brownish red), vermilion (a bright red), bone black and lampblack (both made from carbon), Naples yellow, and flake white. These latter two — Naples yellow and flake white — were dangerous if carelessly used, because they contained lead. If the powder was breathed in or the paint was accidentally taken into the mouth or smeared over an open cut, lead poisoning, a fatal ailment, might result.

During the seventeenth century most of the oil paints used by the limners were either stored in cups that were covered with paper soaked in oil or they were kept in covered cups under water. For the hundred years after about 1700, artists' oil colors were kept in sheeps' bladders. These pouches of color were pierced by a bone pin. If the limner wanted to use a color, he removed the pin and squeezed a small amount of paint onto his thin mixing board, or palette. He then replaced the pin, which sealed the hole and so kept the paint in the bladder reasonably fresh and moist.

*Limners painted their portraits on the best material*
*they could get.*

Often the limner made his own brushes by fastening tufts of strong wild animal fur, such as mink, into the end of a hollow quill. These homemade brushes varied in length and fullness, but hardly ever varied in shape. For the most part, they were round, and had either a sharp or a blunt point.

For a painting surface the limner used the best material he could get. Sometimes portraits were painted on a smoothly planed or sanded board; sometimes on tightly stretched heavy linen or some other strong, heavy fabric.

Most of the limners began a painting by positioning, or posing, their customer in front of them. They would then draw the person directly on the stretched linen or wood with a charred stick or charcoal or a piece of chalk. Once the drawing was finished, the limner would apply his color. Sometimes the limner worked outdoors where the light was good. Usually a small crowd would gather to watch him at work, to offer advice, or to hear him chatter away, relaying all the latest news and gossip. Mostly the limner talked about what a great artist he was, and there were few to doubt him.

Today the limners are remembered chiefly for the stiff-looking portraits they painted. But historical records and the advertisements the limners put in the papers of the time show that they did many other kinds of work to eke out a living. Limners painted maps of the land and pictures of the events and buildings of the day; they made views of the cities and on occasion painted a *landskip*, or landscape; they painted decorative scenes on the walls of houses; they painted ornamental pictures on glass; they decorated coaches; they gilded mirrors; they cleaned paintings; they made copies of other pictures, touched up previously painted works of art, did lettering, and as time went on, tried to teach drawing and painting to others.

Some of their maps and their pictures of the events in the cities are still in existence and are extremely valuable to historians today. Such a painting as that of the British troops encamped on Boston Common when they occupied the city in 1768, painted at that time by Christian Remick, is a priceless record. Portrait painting was probably the most profitable part of the limner's

*The British soldiers encamped on Boston Common. Engraving from a watercolor by Christian Remick in 1768. (New York Public Library, Stokes Collection)*

work, however, and it is mostly the portraits that
have survived.

By the beginning of the eighteenth century,
while the limners plodded along, trying to im-
prove their portraits with each new job, a number of well-trained artists began to arrive in the
colonies. They were not the best that Europe had
to offer, but some of them were far superior to
most of the limners.

Among these skillful professionals was Gusta-
vus Hesselius of Sweden. Even he had to have
some sidelines in order to earn a living. He decorated coaches, painted houses, made signs, did
gilding, and cleaned old pictures in addition to
his portrait painting. From time to time he also
painted historical, religious, and mythological
pictures.

John Smibert, a Scotsman, was another trained
artist from Europe. He came to New England in
1729, bringing with him an Old World skill at
painting that had not been seen in the colonies
before. Smibert settled down in Boston as a portrait painter and very often held exhibitions of
his paintings and the works of others. Both Hes-

*Portrait of the Bermuda Group, by John Smibert.
Oil, 1729. (Yale University Art Gallery)*

selius and Smibert strongly influenced the work of many colonial "face painters," but some limners continued making portraits in the old, flat way.

During the eighteenth century some of the portrait painters became less interested in making an honest likeness of someone and more interested in portraying a person's possessions and his position in life. They made sure that the clothes in the portrait were of suitable grandeur. So a well-to-do lawyer might be pictured richly garbed and surrounded by documents, or a merchant might be shown with his ledger. One portrait still in existence shows Moses Marcy, a merchant, drinking a glass of wine, with his ledger before him and his large house and estate and ship in the background.

This trend of presenting social position in portrait painting is shown by the following advertisement, printed in the *New York Gazette* in 1754.

Lawrence Kilburn, Limner, just arrived from London with Captain Miller, hereby acquaints all Gentlemen and Ladies inclined to

*Portrait of two children in a garden, by John Durand.*
*Oil, c. 1770. (Connecticut Historical Society)*

favour him in having their Pictures drawn,
that he don't doubt of pleasing them in making a true Likeness, and finishing the Drap-
eries in a proper Manner, as also in the choice
of Attitudes, suitable to each Person's Age
and Sex, and giving agreeable Satisfaction,
as he has heretofore done to Gentlemen and
Ladies in London. He may at present be
apply'd to at his lodgings at Mr. Bogart's
near the new Printing Office in Beaver-street.

During almost all of the Colonial period, the
limners stayed mainly in the large towns and
cities. People desiring a portrait sought them out
there. But just before the Revolution the limners
started to move about, looking for work. One limner, John Durand, advertised in New York in
1767, and later painted in Virginia and Connecticut. Some of the limners packed up their possessions and took to a wandering life on the road.
During the summertime they roamed from town
to town and village to village and farm to farm,
charging varying prices for a portrait. Sometimes
they worked for room and board only.

*Portrait of Paul Revere, by John Singleton Copley. Oil on canvas. (Museum of Fine Arts, Boston)*

At times, some of them stayed through the winter with a large family. These limners worked out their lodging by making a portrait of each member of that family. Other limners rented a room in a village for the winter. After advertising, they received enough work in the region to keep them busy until warm weather made it possible for them to take to the road once more.

In time, artistically gifted young colonials such as John Singleton Copley, Gilbert Stuart, and Benjamin West appeared and began to limn (LIM) portraits. All three of these artists went to Europe for further training. Copley and West never returned to America as Stuart did, but they all became skillful portrait painters. They were no longer simple limners. Instead, they became accomplished artists.

As the Revolution moved America toward independence from Great Britain, better trained portrait artists practiced their craft in the colonies. But even after the American Revolution there were still many limners who followed the frontier westward. It was not until the daguerreotype, a forerunner of the photograph, became

popular in the 1840s, that the limners finally disappeared.

During the entire Colonial period the limners were never considered to be as important as the silversmiths or the cabinetmakers. They were looked upon as artisans who worked at an interesting trade, but one that was not absolutely necessary to the comfort and well-being of the colonists. For their part, the limners were not interested either in expressing their feelings about the people they were painting or in expressing what life was like in the New World.

The only thing that interested the limners was to draw or paint the people who hired them exactly as they looked and as full of life as possible. Unfortunately, although many a limner thought that his finished picture was quite lifelike and realistic, the truth is that most of the limners did not know how to use their oil paints to reproduce the natural appearance of their customers. The flat, often ungraceful look of the paintings was unplanned. Yet thanks to these men, we still have today a wealth of portraits giving a telling glimpse of America's people in the earlier, simpler days.

# INDEX

LEONARD EVERETT FISHER is a well-known author-artist whose books include *Alphabet Art, The Great Wall of China, The Tower of London, Marie Curie, Jason and the Golden Fleece, The Olympians, The ABC Exhibit, Sailboat Lost,* and many others.

Often honored for his contribution to children's literature, Mr. Fisher was the recipient of the 1989 Nonfiction Award presented by the *Washington Post* and the Children's Book Guild of Washington for the body of an author's work. In 1991, he received both the Catholic Library Association's Regina Medal and the University of Minnesota's Kerlan Award for the entire body of his work. Leonard Everett Fisher lives in Westport, Connecticut.